HOCKEY: YOU are the COACH

Nate Aaseng

 Lerner Publications Company • Minneapolis

To whomever it was who talked me into writing
the sports column for the *Chips*

LIBRARY OF CONGRESS CATALOGING IN PUBLICATION DATA

Aaseng, Nathan
 Hockey—you are the coach.

 (You are the coach)
 Summary: The reader is invited to make coaching
decisions after being provided with the facts of ten
actual hockey games, most of which are Stanley Cup.
What really happened is presented at the end of each
chapter.
 1. Hockey coaching—Juvenile literature.
 2. Stanley Cup (Hockey)—Juvenile literature.
 [1. Hockey coaching. 2. Stanley Cup (Hockey)]
 I. Title. II. Series: Aaseng, Nathan. You are the
coach.
 GV848.25.A28 1983   796.96'27   82-17170
 ISBN 0-8225-1554-7
 1 2 3 4 5 6 7 8 9 10 92 91 90 89 88 87 86 85 84 83

CONTENTS

Become the Coach! 5

1 The Golden Jet 7

2 Breaking the French Connection 17

3 Canada's Pride at Stake! 25

4 The Offensive Defenseman 36

5 The Old Goalie, or the Older One? 48

6 Rookie vs. Scoring Machine 58

7 Empty Net 68

8 Can the Flyers Afford Penalties? 79

9 The Man Without a Stick 89

10 Team U.S.A. Meets "The Soviet System" 94

Become the Coach!

Hockey fans proudly call their favorite sport the "fastest game in the world." The furious action as players skate up and down the ice at top speed leaves little time for plotting strategies. Yet strategies have often played key roles in championship hockey games. This book puts you behind the bench to see if you can make a difference in a game's outcome. You are the coach for ten actual championship matches.

Because the game of hockey moves so quickly, you will do much of your planning before the game. But things rarely go exactly according to plan, and you will find yourself having to make important decisions between periods. Sometimes, amid the blur of skates on the ice, you must take immediate action.

These decisions may not be easy to make. Some of the most skilled teams in hockey history will present you with great challenges. The 1974 Montreal Canadiens, the 1971 Boston Bruins, the 1972 Soviet National team, and the 1980 New York Islanders are some of the opposing teams that make life tough for a coach. And stars such as Bobby Hull, Bobby Orr, Gil Perreault, and Phil Esposito may provide you with extra headaches.

To give your team a chance against such competition, you're going to have to make plans. You, the coach, will have to decide how to hold on to leads, when to substitute, how to defend, and when to pull the goalie in favor of an extra attacker.

In each chapter, scouting tips will be given as you try to get the edge on your opponent. After you've decided on your strategy, you'll be able to compare your choice with that of a coach in an actual game situation. Like these coaches, you may find that your plans do not always work the way you expect them to. The odds may be so stacked against you that even a good strategy fails. Sometimes, with luck, a questionable decision brings success.

Now it's time to go down to rinkside for some of the most exciting games in hockey history. Find out what kind of hockey coach you are!

1 The Golden Jet

You are coaching
the Montreal Canadiens.

In this 1965 Stanley Cup final, your main worry is
Bobby Hull of the Chicago Black Hawks. You've just
watched "The Golden Jet" singlehandedly knock off
the Detroit Red Wings, favored for the Stanley Cup.
In Chicago's semifinal win over Detroit, Hull scored
8 goals and had 5 assists. Now your team will be
facing Hull and the Black Hawks. What plans
will you make to stop Hull?

Hull is the league's most famous star.

It hardly seems fair that one man should rate at the top in so many hockey skills. Considered the league's fastest skater, Hull can reach speeds of around 30 miles per hour. He also owns the game's hardest shot. Goalies cringe whenever he winds up with his slap shot, which has been clocked at 118 miles per hour! To top it off, Bobby has the strongest upper body in the league. At 5 feet, 10 inches, 195 pounds, he is as solid as a heavyweight boxer.

The Point Anne, Ontario, native turned pro at 18 and burst into the headlines when he scored 50 goals in 1962. Since then, he has been watched closely by other teams. He still gets more than his share of goals and frightens more than his share of goalies. This past season, he scored 39 goals and finished fourth in the NHL (National Hockey League) scoring race with 71 points. Few would argue with Hull's title as the league's Most Valuable Player.

Bobby Hull

The Black Hawks also have several other fine players.

You certainly can't overlook little Stan Mikita, especially since he led the league in scoring. The pesky 5-foot, 9-inch center from Czechoslovakia scored 28 goals and added 59 assists for a total of 87 points. Stan is a hustler and a battler and an expert at keeping control of the puck.

Two other Black Hawks made the top ten in scoring. Pierre Pilote finished eighth, and Phil Esposito ninth. In addition, the Black Hawks signed Hull's brother, Dennis, whose slapshot is said to be equal to Bobby's.

The Black Hawks' most feared warriors: (from left) Stan Mikita, Pierre Pilote, and Bobby Hull

Your Canadiens are a blend of talent, grace, and teamwork.

Although you don't have the hot shooters that Chicago has, two of your men did rank in the top ten in scoring. Claude Provost scored 27 goals and totaled 64 points. Ralph Backstrom added 25 goals and 55 points. Compared to Hull's and Mikita's, these totals pale, but you do have a strong supporting cast of players. Jean Beliveau, Henri Richard, Bobby Rousseau, Dick Duff, and Yvan Cournoyer are among the fine Canadien skaters who swarm all over the rink.

Your defense, however, is not quite at full strength. One of your most reliable defensemen, Jacques Laperriere, is nursing a broken ankle. Fortunately, young Ted Harris seems to be getting more comfortable at that position with each game.

Jean Beliveau

Yvan Cournoyer

You have decided to start Lorne "Gump" Worsley
at goalie instead of Charlie Hodge, who tended
goal for you throughout the season. Worsley came
to you in trade two seasons ago from the New York
Rangers, where he was a goalie for many years.
But Gump was sent down to the minors for a year
and a half and has only recently been brought
back to play with the Canadiens. You are taking
a chance on Worsley in this series against Chicago
because he has not allowed Hull a goal all season.

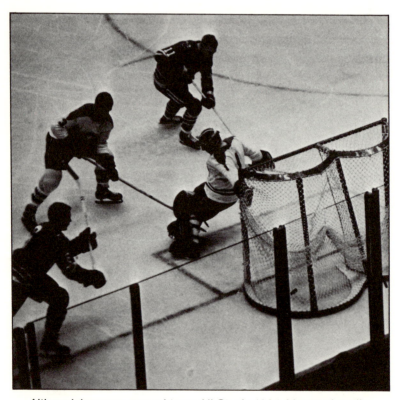

Although he was a second-team All-Star in 1964, Montreal goalie
Charlie Hodge wasn't quick enough here to stop Chicago's
Fred Stanfield (left) from scoring.

There are two main strategies designed to stop hockey superstars.

One of these is the "shadow." Teams sometimes assign one person to "shadow," or stay with, the opposing team's star player. The shadow goes onto the ice whenever the star is playing, whether or not it's the shadow's regular shift.

The other strategy is a checking line. This is a line made up of three forwards with good defensive skills. The entire line takes to the ice whenever the opposing star plays. They do not, however, specifically shadow him.

What's Your Decision?

You are the coach.
To beat the Black Hawks, you must stop Hull.
What strategy will you use?

#1 Have one of your better players shadow Hull.

#2 Have a less skilled man shadow Hull so that you don't have to give up any offensive strength.

#3 Send out a checking line against Hull's line.

#4 Play your usual game without doing anything special about Hull.

Choose the strategy. Then turn the page to find out which strategy the Canadiens' coach chose.

The Canadiens decided to try #1.

Claude Provost was assigned the task of shadowing Hull. The fact that the Canadiens were willing to use their top scorer for this defensive task shows how important they felt Hull was to the Black Hawk offense. Montreal believed that they had enough strength at offense to make up for the loss of Provost.

Here's What Happened!

For seven games, Provost was Hull's tireless companion on the ice. As soon as Bobby's skates touched the ice, Claude was buzzing around him, keeping him away from the puck. The tone for the entire series was set in the first game when a frustrated Hull managed only one shot on goal.

With Hull taken out of the action, Montreal's goalie had an easy time of it. During one of the games, the entire Black Hawk team totaled only 18 shots. Montreal, though, did not do much scoring in the first six games either. As a result, the series was tied at three games apiece. But Montreal continued its shadowing strategy in the final game and easily sealed off the Chicago attack, winning by a score of 4 to 0.

Hull scored only two goals in the entire series, both of them on rare occasions when Provost was not on the ice with him. Provost's great success shadowing Hull almost guaranteed that the great Chicago star would have an unfriendly shadow trailing him for the rest of his career.

Montreal goaltenders Charlie Hodge and Gump Worsley (shown here) held the high-scoring Black Hawk attack to a measly 12 goals in the seven games of the 1965 Stanley Cup finals.

2 Breaking the French Connection

Opposing goalies find Buffalo's French Connection almost criminal. Rene Robert (top), Gil Perreault (left), and Richard Martin together beat enemy netminders 131 times during the 1974-1975 NHL season.

You are coaching
the Philadelphia Flyers.

Unless you want your goalie to be knocked dizzy by flying hockey pucks, you had better figure out a plan to stop the Buffalo Sabres and their high-powered offense. Their top forward line of Gil Perreault, Richard Martin, and René Robert is perhaps the most explosive in the game today. Because of their French-Canadian backgrounds and their slick passing, these three men have become known as the "French Connection."

You have an excellent defensive team, and during the regular season you tied the Sabres in the standings with 113 points. But it will be a special challenge to stop Buffalo's hot line in this 1975 Stanley Cup final. What steps will you take to keep the French Connection out of your goal?

Look at the facts about the Sabres.

Of the three Sabre forwards, left wing Rick Martin has had the most spectacular year. The 5-foot, 11-inch 180-pounder has been the top player at his position in the NHL. He blasted 52 goals this season and assisted on 43 others.

René Robert skates on the right side of the Sabres' attack. At 5 feet, 10 inches and 184 pounds, he is built much like Martin, and his ability to produce goals has been similar as well. Robert scored 40 times during the regular season and received credit for 60 assists. As a reward for his efforts, he was voted a second-team All-Star.

Although center Gil Perreault's statistics are slightly behind those of his linemates, he is the most famous of the three. Opponents and fans have had their eyes on him ever since he scored 38 goals in his rookie season of 1970-1971. He has great moves for a 6-foot-tall 200-pounder, and he totaled 39 goals and 57 assists this season. Despite his size, he is not known as a physical player. In fact, none of the French Connection is known for hard-nosed defensive play.

Unfortunately for your Flyers, the Sabres have several other scoring weapons as well. If you concentrate too hard on stopping the top line, you may leave things wide open for Buffalo's other men. The Sabres were the first team in NHL history to skate six men who each scored more than 30 goals in the same year. In addition to Martin, Robert, and Perreault, they have center Don Luce, who scored 33, and rookie right wing Danny Gare and left wing Rick Dudley, who each added 31.

Buffalo also keeps several large and aggressive defensemen in the game to take the pressure off their scorers. Jerry Korab and Jim Schoenfeld both use their 220 pounds to protect their side of the ice.

Rick Dudley

Don Luce

Danny Gare

Now check out the strengths of your own team.

Your number-one line is led by the courageous little battler Bobby Clarke. Clarke led the league in assists with 89, scored 27 goals, and generally made life miserable for opponents with his defensive work. Most experts consider him the best checker in the league. Many of his passes have set up Reggie Leach for scores. Leach scored 45 goals but is weak on defense. The second line, centered by Rick MacLeish, can also put the puck in the net. MacLeish tallied 38 goals this season.

You also possess a whole benchful of bruising forwards who don't score much but can play good defense. Dave Schultz and Bob Kelly are two of

Flyer captain Bobby Clarke overcame diabetes to become one of hockey's top players. In 1974-75, Clarke led the NHL in assists with 89, was named First All-Star Team center, and won the Hart Trophy as the league's Most Valuable Player.

the more infamous members of this group. But they also put your team at a disadvantage with all the penalties they take for overaggressive play.

Your goalie is Bernie Parent. Bernie is so good that yours is one of the few teams that does not alternate two goalies. Parent recorded 12 shutouts during the year and allowed an average of only 2.03 goals per game. Not surprisingly, this was good enough to win a second-straight Vezina Trophy, awarded to the goalie allowing fewest total goals in the season.

What's Your Decision?

You are the coach.
To take the Stanley Cup, you must stop the French Connection.
How will you overcome these three stars?

#1 Overwhelm them with fresh skaters and try to tire them out by sending in several line changes during each French Connection shift.

#2 Put a "shadow" on Rick Martin.

#3 Send out a checking line with people like Schultz and Kelly whenever they are on the ice.

#4 Match Clarke's line against them.

#5 Don't worry about them, and figure that Parent is good enough to stop them.

Choose the strategy. Then turn the page to find out which strategy the Flyers' coach chose.

The Flyers decided on #1.

Even though Parent was a great goalie, Philadelphia still was not about to let the Sabres pepper
him with their usual volley of shots (#5). There
was no point in shadowing Martin or any other
Buffalo player since there were so many of them who
could score (#2). Philadelphia decided that wave
after wave of fresh skaters would be the best choice.
This would spread the task of stopping the Connection to a lot of players rather than to just one
player or one line (#3 and #4). The Flyers knew that
Buffalo would want to take full advantage of the
French Connection's skills by leaving them on
the ice for long shifts. The use of three lines skating
all out during one French Connection shift could
wear out the Buffalo stars.

Here's What Happened!

When Perreault, Martin, and Robert took their first turn on the ice, they found themselves battling different Flyers every 30 seconds. Philadelphia skated three lines during each of the French Connection's first two shifts.

The Sabres were a little unsettled by this. The Buffalo club that scored a team-record 354 goals during the year could manage only 12 scores in the six-game final against Philadelphia. In four of those six games, the Flyers won, holding their opponents to one goal or less. The French Connection was stopped, the rest of the Sabres were unable to take over the scoring, and the Flyers won their second-straight Stanley Cup title.

Next page: Bobby Clarke proudly carries the Stanley Cup, symbol of hockey supremacy, as the Flyers skate their victory lap around the rink. Philadelphia broke the French Connection and defeated the Sabres in six games.

3 Canada's Pride at Stake!

You are coaching the 1972 Team Canada.

This is a group of NHL All-Stars who were selected to play in a special series of games against the Soviet Union. No one knew how the Soviets, the kings of Olympic hockey, would do against a team of Canadian professionals. But it had always been taken for granted that the Canadians played the best hockey in the world, and in this series they were expected to give the Soviets some hockey lessons.

To everyone's shock, it's been the Russians who have done most of the instructing early in the series. Now, with only two out of eight games left to play, the Soviets lead three games to two with one tie.

The North American fans are outraged, and the pressure on you is fierce. You must come up with a plan that will help you combat the stunning speed of the Soviet skaters. Their advantage in speed is most glaring at the center position. Your once-confident All-Stars have been regularly beaten in races to the puck. Of the five centers on your roster who have played in this series, only Bobby Clarke and occasionally Phil Esposito have been effective. What can you do to strengthen the center position?

Take a close look at the centers on your roster.

The six centers together have managed a total of six goals in six games.

	Goals	Assists	Points
Esposito	3	4	7
Clarke	2	4	6
Ratelle	1	0	1
Mikita	0	1	1
Berenson	0	1	1
Dionne	(has not played)		

These figures don't reflect the production you expected from players who during last year's NHL season sported the statistics shown on the next page:

	Goals	Assists	Points
Esposito	66*	67	133*
Ratelle	46	63	109
Clarke	35	46	81
Dionne	28	49	77
Berenson	28	41	69
Mikita	26	39	65

*led league

Phil Esposito   Jean Ratelle   Bobby Clarke

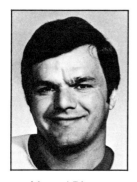

Marcel Dionne   Red Berenson   Stan Mikita

27

Clarke, a three-year veteran, has surprised hockey experts by being the top center on the team so far. Teamed with Toronto Maple Leaf wings Paul Henderson and Ron Ellis, Clarke has helped check the Soviets' top line and has contributed points as well.

Esposito has been bogged down lately by the Soviets' checking line. At 6 feet, 3 inches, 205 pounds, Phil is one of the larger forwards in the game and is most effective when he plants himself in front of the opposing goals. From there he whacks in rebounds, passes, and loose pucks for goals. Phil is a great competitor, and it has been a full-time job for the Soviets to move him out of position. But you need even more goals from him than he has been producing.

Jean (the French word for John) Ratelle is a graceful, smooth player who has been especially disappointing in this series. It sometimes takes him a while to set up a play, and the Soviets have not given him one spare second. Veterans Stan Mikita and Red Berenson have been clearly outskated during most of their shifts. Dionne may have the speed to challenge some of the Russian skaters, but he has had only one year of NHL experience.

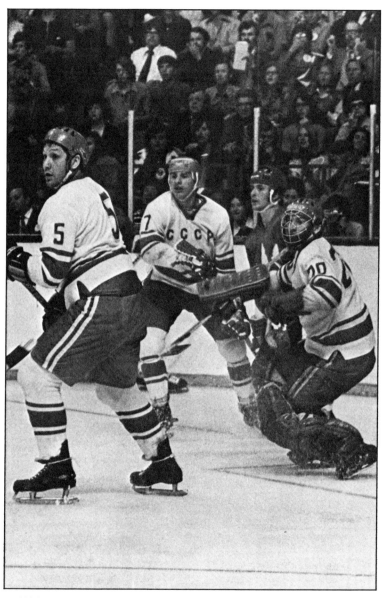

With heads-up play, smooth skating, and crisp passing, the Soviets have taken a commanding lead into the seventh game of their series with Team Canada.

Now look at the strengths and weaknesses of the Soviets.

There doesn't seem to be any way to get the Soviets to slow down the game to a comfortable pace. You tried skating four forward lines in the first game, but that left you with only five defensemen. These five could not stand up to the Soviet pressure and allowed seven goals. You have had some success dumping the puck in the corners and out-muscling the Soviets for control of the puck. But they continue to rush the puck back to the other end for breakaways.

Generally, the Soviet team is in far better shape than your team. Team Canada had only two and a half weeks of practice before the series started. Since the contest is taking place in the NHL's off-season, some players could have used more practice time. The Soviets, on the other hand, are in top condition, as always.

They do, however, seem to have a weakness on defense in their own zone. They are also limited by a very rigid pattern of offense and defense. Whereas each NHL player has his own style of play, the Soviets all tend to play a similar brand of hockey.

What's Your Decision?

You are the coach.

In order to save your pride, you must win the final two games.

What can you do to get better play at the center position?

#1 Skate three lines with Clarke, Esposito, and the newcomer Dionne at center. Put Ratelle, Berenson, and Mikita on the bench.

#2 Skate four lines with Clarke, Esposito, and veterans Ratelle and Mikita at center. Use five defensemen instead of six.

#3 Skate four lines with Clark and Ratelle centering one line each and ask Esposito to take double duty by centering <u>two</u>. This allows you to keep six defensemen.

#4 Skate three lines with Clarke, Esposito, and Ratelle at center, but give Clarke and Esposito longer shifts.

Choose the play. Then turn the page to find out which play the Team Canada coach chose.

Team Canada decided on #3.

After the first disastrous game, Canada would not even think about playing with only five defensemen (#2). Dionne was untested, and the coach did not want to experiment with him so late in the series (#1). This left choices #3 and #4. The Russians were in better shape than the Canadians, so it did not make sense to put Clarke's and Esposito's lines out for longer shifts. These six men had trouble keeping up as it was.

Esposito, however, was one man who might be able to handle more playing time. Because of his size and determination, it probably took more effort for the opposition to try and move him away from the goal than it took for him to stay there. More importantly, this would allow Phil to take several shifts free from the Soviet's checking line. The Soviets wouldn't change their rigid game plan just to keep up with Phil.

Ratelle was called on to center the third line simply because no one else had shown he could do a better job.

Here's What Happened!

In a classic display of stubborn will, Esposito
refused to be shoved out of his position in front of
the goal. During one stretch in the first period of
game number seven, he stayed on the ice for over
five minutes, while his linemates changed twice.
Phil's effort paid off with two goals in the first period,
sparking a 4 to 3 win for Canada.

In the final game, the Soviets threatened to
rout the Canadians as they scored five goals in
the first two periods. But Esposito, with a goal, and
Ratelle, with two assists, worked to keep their
team within two goals.

Two minutes into the third period, Esposito again
took his position near the goal as teammate Frank
Mahovlich skated in with the puck. Phil held his
ground long enough to bat down a high pass from
Mahovlich and shoved it into the net. Ten minutes
later, he fed a pass to Yvan Cournoyer, who scored
the tying goal. Then, with less than a minute
remaining in the game, Phil again stayed on the
ice while his linemates went off. On a final rush into
the Soviet end, he assisted Paul Henderson's goal,
which won the game 6 to 5 and salvaged the series
4 games to 3 with one tie. Esposito's gutsy performance saved the pride of the NHL from the
high-powered Soviet team.

Phil Esposito made an immovable fixture of himself in front of the Soviet net during the series' last two games. Largely because of his huge presence there, Team Canada players were spared the wrath of their hockey-crazed countrymen.

4 The Offensive Defenseman

Bobby Orr: the best defenseman in hockey

You are coaching
the St. Louis Blues.

This is your third-straight year in the Stanley Cup finals, but that record is not as impressive as it first sounds. Your Western Division has been so much weaker than the more established Eastern Division that the finals between the divisional champions have been a joke. In each of the last two championships, you were beaten by Montreal in four straight games. To be honest, you would probably be the underdog against <u>any</u> Eastern Division team in this 1970 final.

And to make matters worse, this is not just <u>any</u> team you are playing. Your opponents, the Boston Bruins, are hungry for a title after going almost thirty years without one. With their superstar defenseman Bobby Orr, Boston poses the biggest problem in pro hockey. What plans will you make to stop Orr?

You know that Orr has singlehandedly turned the hockey world upside down.

Before Bobby came along, a defenseman was mainly concerned with protecting his goaltender and with working the puck out of the defensive end. He would let the forwards take care of most of the scoring. Orr, however, often acts like a fourth forward. He can so dominate a game that he will lead rushes on the opposing goal and still skate back fast enough to cover his position on defense.

Bobby completely defied hockey logic when he won the Art Ross Trophy this season as the league's top scorer. Never before had a defenseman even

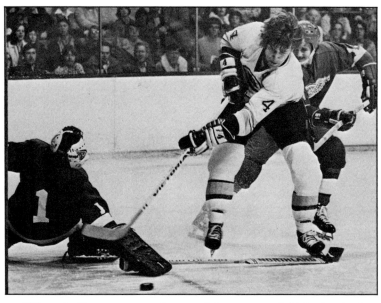

Although it's uncommon to see defensemen right in front of their opponents' crease, Bobby Orr's offensive style of play often took him just there. This Red Wing netminder looks back helplessly as Orr slides the puck past him.

come close to winning that award. But Orr's rink-length dashes and quick, hard shots brought him 33 goals and 87 assists, and he finished more than 20 points ahead of his nearest rival.

The Port Sound, Ontario native is one of the game's strongest players as well. Boston does not hesitate to play him in any situation, whether it's killing penalties or taking his shift on the power play.

In play-off competition this year, Orr is nearing another series of records. He has totaled 8 goals and 7 assists and is almost certain to break many play-off records for scoring by a defenseman.

Boston also has Esposito, the second-best scorer in the game, plus a strong supporting cast of players.

Phil Esposito gets many of his goals by batting in the puck after mad scrambles in front of the goal. Envious opponents like to criticize these scores by calling them "garbage goals." But even though these goals are not particularly pretty to watch, they still count. This past season, Phil notched 43 goals and had 56 assists, finishing second to Orr in the scoring race.

In addition, four other Bruins totaled more than 20 goals. Johnny Bucyk scored 31, John McKenzie 29, Ken Hodge 25, and Fred Stanfield 23. The offensive-minded Bruins are feeling confident, having just polished off the Chicago Black Hawks in four straight games.

Brother faces brother as Boston center Phil Esposito fires a
shot on Chicago goalie Tony Esposito. Black Hawk enforcer
Keith Magnuson, down on the ice, looks on.

40

Johnny Bucyk

Ken Hodge

Fred Stanfield

John McKenzie

41

Your Blues, on the other hand, are mainly a collection of unknown players.

The only two who could be considered stars are Red Berenson and Phil Goyette. The crafty "Red Baron" has spent some time with more established clubs, such as the Montreal Canadiens, before joining the Blues. A fine player both offensively and defensively, Berenson scored 33 goals and had 39 assists for a 72-point total. With 29 goals and 49 assists for 78 points, Goyette topped the team in scoring. The rest of your forwards, however, do not cause Boston much worry.

Red Berenson

42

You have an unusual situation on defense in that three of your defensemen—Barclay, Bob, and Bill Plager—are brothers. All three are known as solid checkers. But Barclay and fellow defenseman Al Arbour are both hurt, and that means your defense is hurting, too.

You are one of the few teams that carries three goalies. That is because two of them, Glenn Hall and Jacques Plante, are old-timers who could end their careers at any minute. They are proven play-off performers who are still capable of playing well, but probably not well enough to hold the Bruins off without help.

What's Your Decision?

You are the coach.
You'd like, for once, to take the Stanley Cup.
What can your less-talented team do to stop Orr and the Bruins?

#1 Keep the puck away from Orr's side of the rink whenever possible.

#2 Put a shadow on Orr even though he is a defenseman.

#3 Play your usual game and don't concentrate on Orr.

Choose the strategy. Then turn the page to find out what strategy the Blues' coach chose.

The Blues decided on choice #2.

It was totally unheard of for any team to put a shadow on another team's defenseman. But the Blues figured that since Orr had such great scoring skill, an unusual strategy was necessary. Many teams had tried to keep the puck away from him, but no one could claim that any strategy had worked. Since no one had yet found a sure-fire method for stopping Orr, the Blues were willing to experiment with yet another strategy.

Here's What Happened!

In the first game, Jim Roberts was assigned the task of stopping Orr. If you look at some of the figures for that game, it appears as though the strategy worked. Orr was held to four shots on goal and did not score. Meanwhile, his shadow (Roberts) scored for St. Louis in the second period. But in slowing down Orr, the Blues gave the Bruin forwards much more room to move, and Boston won the game 6 to 1. Although Orr himself did not score, he was on the ice for five of his team's goals, three of them by Bucyk.

In game two, it became even more obvious that the Blues' strategy was hopeless. Boston outshot St. Louis 16 to 5 in the first period. With Ed Westfall scoring twice, the Bruins moved out to a 3-0 lead.

That was enough to convince the Blues' coach to call off the shadow during intermission. Boston went on to win, 6 to 2, and then took game number three by a score of 4 to 1. During each of those games, Orr was held scoreless.

St. Louis had their best showing of the series in the fourth game, and they tied the Bruins 3 to 3 at the end of regulation time. But just 30 seconds into overtime, Orr saw an opening and charged recklessly toward the net. He drew close to the goal and fired a shot. Trying desperately to stop Orr, a St. Louis defenseman tripped Bobby and sent him flying. But the puck hit the back of the net anyway, and the game was won as Bobby sailed through the air.

Perhaps the best way to evaluate the Blues' shadowing strategy is to compare Boston's scoring before and after St. Louis called off the shadow. Boston outscored the Blues 9 to 1 in the four periods Orr was being shadowed. During the next eight periods, the Bruins outscored the Blues only 10 to 6.

Next page: Phil Esposito is stopped at the goal-mouth by veteran Jacques Plante in action from game one of the Blues-Bruins Stanley Cup final. The Blues' Jim Roberts trails Esposito. Though the St. Louis goalie was successful here, Boston outscored the Blues 20-7 for the series.

5 The Old Goalie, or the Older One?

Both Johnny Bower (left) and Terry Sawchuk
have stopped enough pucks to be seeing them
in their dreams. Has one of these old men
just about run out of saves?

You are coaching the Toronto Maple Leafs.

It's the semifinal round of the 1967 Stanley Cup play-offs, and it's your bad fortune to have drawn the Chicago Black Hawks as your opponents. The Chicago team breezed into first place this season with a 41-17-12 record, while you staggered into the play-offs at 32-27-11.

You have been criticized for staying with a large group of old veterans instead of rebuilding the club with young blood. Nowhere is this more obvious than in the goal. Terry Sawchuk is 38 years old and in his twentieth pro season—and he is the <u>younger</u> of your two goalies! Forty-two-year-old Johnny Bower alternates with Sawchuk in the nets.

Bower had been scheduled to start the series, but a painful finger injury caused him to sit out in favor of Sawchuk. Terry was blasted by the Black Hawks 5 to 2 in the first game, but he then settled down to post a pair of wins by identical 3 to 1 scores. In game four, Chicago evened the best-of-seven series by beating Sawchuk 4 to 3.

After blocking pucks for nearly 20 years, Sawchuk is not quite as durable as he once was. He admitted after the fourth game that he was tired and in need of rest. Bower's finger seemed better, so you decided to play him and give Sawchuk the rest. But in the first period of game number five, Bower had trouble stopping the puck. Even though they outplayed the Black Hawks, your Maple Leafs were lucky to escape the period with a 2-2 tie.

Your hopes for an upset depend on a good performance from one of these aging players. Who should you send out for the second period?

Johnny Bower

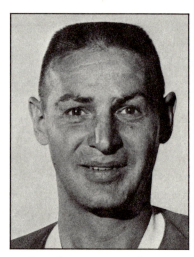
Terry Sawchuk

You know that both players have fine records.

Sawchuk is considered one of the finest goalies in the history of the NHL. He has won or shared the Vezina Trophy four times, has been named first-team All-Star three times, and has been listed on the second All-Star team four times. He is described as a crouching goalie who is an expert at cutting down the shooting angles of his opponents.

But this has not been one of Terry's more successful years. He had wanted to retire before the season but was talked out of it. Then, shortly after the season began, he had back problems that were so severe he ended up in the hospital. Terry appeared in only 27 games all season, and his stamina may be worn down because of lack of playing time.

Bower is an unusual case. He was a true late bloomer, having spent 12 of his first 13 seasons in the minor leagues. He had given up his hopes of ever making it to the NHL, as had the New York Rangers, his original team. But in 1961 he finally ended up in Toronto, where at age 36 he made a name for himself when he was selected to the first team of All-Stars. Johnny led the Maple Leafs to three straight Stanley Cup titles from 1961 to 1963 and has collected two Vezina trophies in his career. He is a stand-up goalie and still displays excellent reactions and athletic ability despite injuries that would have caused most people to quit the game.

You are also aware of the Black Hawks' firepower.

For many years, Chicago has enjoyed a reputation as the best group of shooters in hockey. This season has been no exception as they scored a league record of 264 goals. With his sizzling slap shot, Bobby Hull topped the NHL with 52 goals, and center Stan Mikita finished first in the scoring race with 97 points. Other feared Black Hawk shooters include Phil Esposito and Dennis Hull. These fine shooters are fast to take advantage of any weakness the goaltender might have.

A lot of hockey teams would like to have this woman's talent for raising top-notch players. Mrs. Hull's boys, Bobby (left) and Dennis, own two of the hardest shots in hockey.

Stan Mikita

What's Your Decision?

> You are the coach.
> It's time to take to the ice for the second period.
> **Who will you send in to face the Black Hawks?**
>
> **#1** Sawchuk
> **#2** Bower

Choose the goalie. Then turn the page to find out which goalie the Maple Leafs' coach chose.

The Maple Leafs sent out #1, Sawchuk.

Bower did not seem to be playing his best game. Even though his injury seemed to have improved, it might still be affecting him. Against a team as explosive as Chicago, Toronto felt they didn't want to find out the hard way whether or not Bower had actually recovered.

Sawchuk may have been tired, but this was Stanley Cup action. A team could not afford to rest a tired player if it meant risking a loss. The Maple Leafs hoped the excitement of play-off action would help Terry find an extra reserve of strength. In addition, his skill at cutting down the shooting angles could be especially effective against a shooting team like the Black Hawks.

Here's What Happened!

The Black Hawks wasted no time testing Sawchuk's reflexes. They stormed the net furiously, only to be stopped by one of Terry's most brilliant games. Chicago star Bobby Hull said afterwards that it was the most frustrating game he could remember. It seemed to him that his team had had enough chances to win the game many times over. But Sawchuk did not allow another goal in the game, and Toronto won it, 4 to 2. Sawchuk also worked the next game of the series and the Maple Leafs knocked the favored Black Hawks out of the play-offs.

In the Stanley Cup finals series against Montreal, it was Bower's turn to come through for the Maple Leafs. He shut out the Canadiens in one game and stopped 60 shots in another overtime win before yet another injury forced him to the bench. Sawchuk finished that series, which Toronto won, four games to two, for the Stanley Cup trophy.

Next page: With the pressure on, 38-year-old Terry Sawchuk sparkled. Here in Stanley Cup competition, he stops a Chicago shooter at point-blank range.

6 Rookie vs. Scoring Machine

Phil Esposito

Wayne Cashman

Ken Dryden

VS.

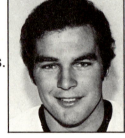

Ken Hodge

John McKenzie

John Bucyk

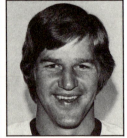

Bobby Orr

What chance has young Ken Dryden against these veteran sharpshooters from Boston?

You are coaching
the Montreal Canadiens.

It is your bad fortune to have been paired against the Boston Bruins in your opening series of the 1971 Stanley Cup play-offs. The Bruins are the defending champions, and they easily topped the league standings during the regular season. They have been scoring goals so fast they might short out the red goal lights.

Your Canadiens are a fine veteran team and finished third in a tough division, but they are not in the same class as Boston. Some hockey experts thought you had been scared witless by the mighty Bruins. They could see no other explanation for your having put Ken Dryden in goal for the series. It is an understatement to refer to Dryden as a rookie. His total experience in the NHL comes to just <u>six</u> games.

Somehow, you have held on to tie the series three games to three. Dryden has played well in starting every game and was minding the nets again at the start of this game. Playing better than they had all season, your Canadiens shot off to a 4-1 lead after two periods. But the proud and skillful Bruins, faced with elimination from the play-offs, have come out furiously in this period. It has taken them just over one minute to cut your lead to 4-2.

Obviously, Boston is going to throw at you everything they can in this final period. What will you do to stop them?

You know what to expect from Boston.

The Bruins dominated the league in an offensive show that broke all records. They broke 37 individual and team scoring records for the NHL, most of them by wide margins. No team has come close to the Bruins' total of 399 goals, an average of 5 per game. A look at the Boston players in the NHL's list of top scorers shows how far ahead of the rest of the league they are:

	Goals	Assists	Points
1. Phil Esposito	76	76	152
2. Bobby Orr	37	102	139
3. John Bucyk	51	65	116
4. Ken Hodge	43	62	105

5. Bobby Hull (Chicago)	44	52	96
6. Norm Ullman (Toronto)	34	51	85
7. Wayne Cashman	21	58	79
8. John McKenzie	31	46	77
9. Dave Keon (Toronto)	38	38	76
10. Jean Beliveau (Montreal)	25	51	76
11. Fred Stanfield	24	52	76

There is no sense in concentrating on one particular Bruin or on one Bruin offensive line, since everyone but the trainer seems to be among the league leaders in points. Both of the Bruins' top lines are simply overwhelming. Esposito centered a line with Hodge and Cashman that set a record for one line with 140 goals. When they left the ice, there was hardly a drop in talent as the Stanfield/Bucyk/McKenzie line took over.

In addition to all those great forwards, Boston relies on the game's top defenseman, Bobby Orr. Many consider Orr to be the greatest ever to play the game. When the Bruins are on the offensive, defenseman Orr displays such fine offensive skills that some consider him a fourth attacking forward.

Bobby Orr

Your Canadiens are solid, but not nearly as spectacular as the Bruins.

Like all Canadien teams of the past, this one excels in fast skating and slick passing. Although they can play fine defense, they are not known as a physical club.

The story of goalie Ken Dryden is one of the most unusual to come out of pro hockey. At 6 feet, 4 inches, he stands almost a head higher than the average pro goalie. Dryden's size gives him quite an advantage. He fills up quite a bit of the cage with his 210 pounds, and his long arms can snare shots most goalies can't reach. At the same time, he seems to be nearly as quick as the smaller goalies.

Dryden, a three-time All-American at Cornell University, is actually more at home in the classroom than on the ice. His law school studies have often pushed his hockey career into the background.

Ken was called up to the Canadiens from a minor league team late in the season. He allowed only nine goals in his six starts and impressed you enough so that you gambled with him in this series. The pressure of the play-offs is far greater than in the regular season, though. And it may be asking quite a bit to expect an inexperienced youngster to fend off the frenzied Bruins' attack in a do-or-die final period.

You also have an experienced goalie, Rogatien Vachon. Vachon has been sitting on the bench, wondering what Dryden is doing playing in his place. In his four full seasons in the league, Rogy has always kept his goals-allowed average at under three per game. He has a history of doing even better than that in the play-offs. The more standard-sized Vachon (5 foot, 7 inches) allowed 1.42 goals per game in the eight play-off games of 1969.

You must also realize that there is danger in letting up when you have a lead. Boston found that out in the second game of your series. They let a 5 to 1 lead evaporate and finally lost to you, 7 to 5.

What's Your Decision?

You are the coach.
Boston has begun to rally and is threatening your lead.
What is your strategy for the rest of the game?

#1 Keep the pressure on with your usual, fast-skating game.

#2 Protect your lead by playing defensively.

#3 Switch goaltenders to bring in the play-off-tested Vachon.

Choose the strategy. Then turn the page to find out which strategy the Canadiens' coach chose.

Montreal chose strategy #2.

For the remainder of the game, the Canadiens rarely ventured into the Boston end of the rink (#1). They held back in their own end, and when they got the puck they often just dumped it into the Boston end rather than rush the net. It was a little late to switch over suddenly to Vachon in goal after Dryden had played the first 6⅔ games (#3). So far, Ken had held up well and Montreal counted on him to handle the pressure in the final period.

Here's What Happened!

The Canadiens' defensive plan did not stop Boston from unleashing a brisk attack. The high-scoring Bruins fired 18 shots on goal in the final period while Montreal fired only 7. If it hadn't been for Dryden's spectacular play, this defensiveness might have proved costly to the Canadiens. Dryden continually thwarted the Bruins, especially Phil Esposito. Phil often pounded his stick in despair after a Dryden save. He later complained about Ken's "giraffe" arms that seemed to reach every shot. For the game, Ken stopped 46 of 48 shots as Montreal upset Boston with a 4 to 2 win.

Dryden continued to do well in the play-offs. Montreal advanced to the finals against Chicago and faced a situation almost identical to the one described above. In the third period of the deciding game, Dryden held up under a barrage of shots as Montreal again went into a defensive shell. Ken beat the Black Hawks and was awarded the Conn Smythe Trophy as the Most Valuable Player in the play-offs.

It's once . . .

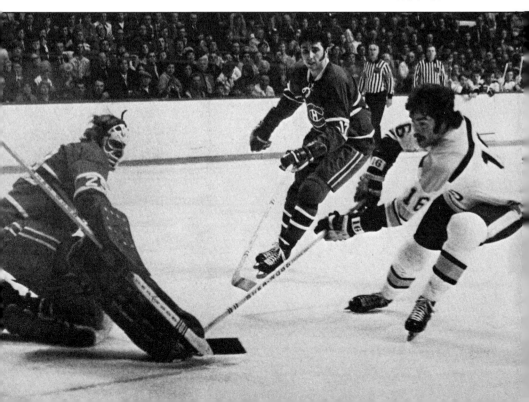

...twice, three times and Boston's out of the play-offs, as Ken Dryden foils Derek Sanderson (previous page), Bobby Orr (above), and Johnny Bucyk (opposite) to end Bruin hopes.

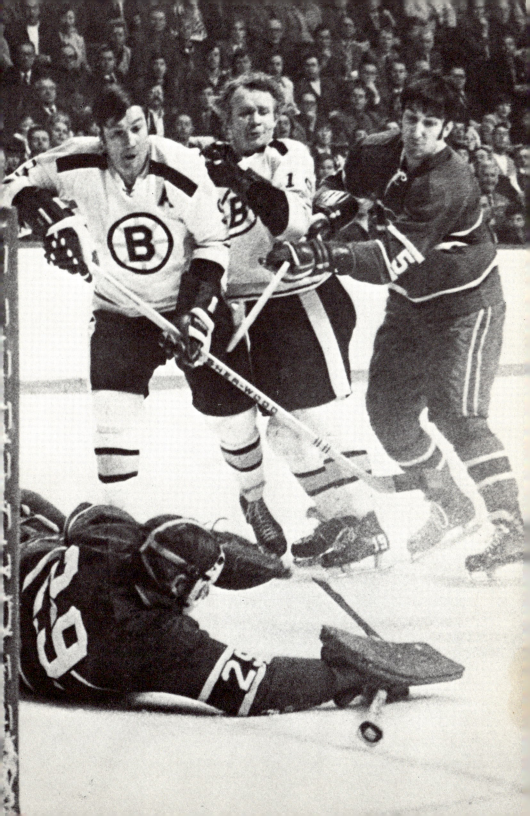

7 Empty Net

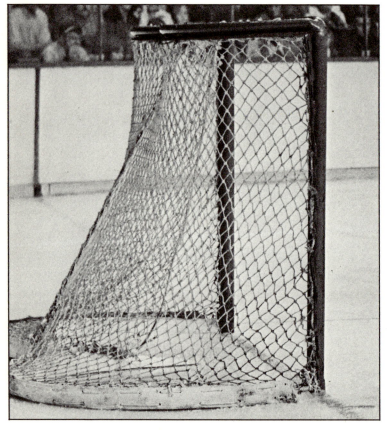

What could be more defenseless?

You are coaching
the New York Rangers.

Your third-place Rangers have a chance to gain some revenge against the Montreal Canadiens by knocking off the defending champs in the first round of the 1974 play-offs. The Montreal Canadiens have captured 17 championships, including most recently the 1973 win over the Chicago Black Hawks. Despite the presence of many fine players, your frustrated Rangers have not won a Stanley Cup title since 1940. You have matched strides with Montreal by winning two of the first four games of the best-of-seven series.

Game number five has been a struggle ever since Montreal's Henri Richard scored just 49 seconds after the opening face-off. Later in the period, Bruce MacGregor tied it for you, and then the defenses took over. Despite numerous break-aways in the game, neither team could score again until well into the third period. Then Murray Wilson scored a goal, pushing the Canadiens back into the lead.

Your Rangers cannot come up with the tying goal, and you watch nervously as the clock ticks down. There is now just under a minute left in the game. As a whistle blows for a face-off in the Montreal end, you wonder if there is any way you can get that tying goal.

Near the end of the game, the losing team sometimes "pulls" the goalie.

The goalie skates to the bench and is replaced by a sixth attacking player. This is a desperate measure since it leaves your net wide open. But with only 56 seconds to go you _are_ in a desperate position.

The idea is that six skaters can control the puck and keep it in the offensive end as though they were on a power play. Teams score far more frequently with a manpower advantage than when both teams play at full strength.

More often than not, though, the other team gets an easy goal or two when you pull the goalie. All it takes to get a goal is a quick burst up the ice and a long, soft shot. This can quickly take the pressure off the leading team for the final minute of the game.

Although the puck is now deep in the Montreal end, your team does not have control. If Montreal wins the face-off, they would have a great chance to gain a safe lead by scoring into an empty net.

Review the Canadiens' strengths.

Montreal sends out a rugged defense led by
Guy LaPointe, Serge Savard, and Larry Robinson.
These skaters, each over 6 feet tall and weighing
more than 200 pounds, are three big reasons why
you have scored only one goal in this game.

Veteran forward Yvan Cournoyer is nicknamed
"The Roadrunner," which tells you how quickly
he can dash down the ice. Guy Lafleur, Jacques
Lemaire, and Steve Shutt are other star members
of a team that has broken away from your defensemen several times in the game.

The Canadiens, perhaps thinking back to 1971
and Ken Dryden, are playing a rookie, Michel
(Bunny) Larocque, in goal. Larocque started 27
games this season and allowed 2.89 goals per game.

Montreal goalie Bunny Larocque sprawls to make a stick save.

Finally, take into account your own players.

You have not had any explosive scorers this season. In fact, only Brad Park, a defenseman, ranked in the top ten in scoring in the NHL. Park finished ninth with 82 points on 25 goals and 57 assists. You do have good scoring balance with several capable lines. Hustling skaters such as Walt Tkaczuk, Bruce MacGregor, and the slick Jean Ratelle are seasoned pros. Center Pete Stemkowski has also played well in this series and has been remarkably successful at winning face-offs.

With captain Vic Hadfield sidelined due to injury, you are missing some of your offensive power. Hadfield's replacement is Ron Harris, who has scored only one goal in the past five months.

Walt Tkaczuk

Brad Park

Ed Giacomin

Your goalie, Ed Giacomin, is skating circles nervously while waiting for your signal. On the other end of the ice, the referee is moving to the face-off circle.

What's Your Decision?

You are the coach.
With 56 seconds remaining in the game, you are one goal behind.
What will you do?

#1 Pull the goalie now.

#2 Wait to see who wins the face-off before pulling him.

#3 Wait until 30 seconds are left before pulling him.

#4 Leave the goalie in and replace defensemen with forwards for extra scoring strength.

Choose the play. Then turn the page to see which play the Rangers' coach chose.

The Rangers decided on #1.

Desperate for a score, New York chose to put all their men in the Montreal end to help control the puck. Stemkowski had been handling face-offs as easily as if his opponent had no stick, and the Rangers counted on him to get control. New York knew that in order to score they would need the extra attacker for all of the 56 seconds that remained.

Here's What Happened!

Stemkowski again came through in the face-off circle, and the extra forward helped the Rangers keep the puck in the Montreal end. Still, Montreal kept the Rangers from scoring for 15 seconds, then 25, then 35. Finally, however, with 16 seconds left in the game, Brad Park fed a pass to Bruce MacGregor. MacGregor slammed the puck into the net for his second goal of the game, and the score forced Montreal into an overtime period.

It took New York four minutes of overtime play before they finished off the disappointed Canadiens. Ron Harris came up with one of his rare goals and gave his team a thrilling 3-2 win.

In the very next game, it was New York who held a one-goal lead with a minute to play. Just as the Rangers had done, Montreal chose to pull their goalie at that point. The strategy backfired for Montreal, however, as New York's Stemkowski scored two of the easiest goals of his life on an empty net. The Rangers won, 5 to 2. Although New York did not win the Stanley Cup that year, at least they had the thrill of knocking the defending champs out of the play-offs.

An important but often overlooked part of hockey is the face-off. At no time are face-offs more important than at the end of a tight game. Knowing this, the Ranger coach has sent Pete Stemkowski (opposite) into the face-off circle to win the draw.

8 Can the Flyers Afford Penalties?

Philadelphia captain Bobby Clarke typifies the aggressive spirit
of the Flyers. Here he sits in the penalty box, blood running
from a cut around his left eye.

You are coaching
the Philadelphia Flyers.

Your opponents in the semifinals of the 1980 Stanley Cup championship are the Minnesota North Stars. The North Stars are currently the hottest thing on ice in the league. They beat four-time defending champion Montreal three times on the Canadiens' home ice to knock them out of the quarterfinals. Now they have won the first game of this semifinal contest by taking a 6-5 decision over you on your home rink.

The North Stars are known as a fast-skating team while your Flyers have long held a reputation as an aggressive, hard-checking group. Your team has both the skill and the strength to shatter the North Stars' confidence with aggressive checking. Such aggressive play, however, can result in penalties. Can you afford the risk of giving the speedy North Stars power plays because of over-aggressive play?

Minnesota's players are among the youngest in the league.

Leading scorer Steve Payne is only 21, and other top point producers such as Bobby Smith and Steve Christoff are 22. Few of the Stars have had much Stanley Cup play-off experience. Yet the North Stars have just beaten the traditionally swift-skating Canadiens at their own game.

The North Stars field an effective power play unit. With 75 power play goals, they ranked fourth in the league this season. Payne alone tallied 16 times when the Stars had a one-man advantage, and veteran Al MacAdam chipped in 13 power play goals.

Minnesota relies more on finesse than on physical play. In penalty minutes this year, they ranked 13th out of 21 teams in the league.

Opposite: Can Philadelphia's Broad Street Bullies risk taking penalties against Minnesota's potent power play, featuring (clockwise from top left) Al MacAdam, Bobby Smith, Steve Payne, and Steve Christoff?

Your Flyers play a hard-hitting game.

This is the style that brought you two straight Stanley Cup titles in 1974 and 1975. Since then, you have remained at the top of the league in penalties, leading the National Hockey League in 1979-80 with 1,844 minutes in penalties. You also finished first in the standings with 116 points, six more than Buffalo, the next highest finisher.

At times, your aggressiveness has cost you. During the season, your Flyers found themselves short-handed 381 times and gained a power-play advantage only 270 times. As a result, your team gave up 79 power-play goals while scoring only 44.

The number of power-play goals your team allowed would have been even greater than 79 if it weren't for the fine play of the penalty-killing units. Bobby Clarke, Bill Barber, Mel Bridgeman,

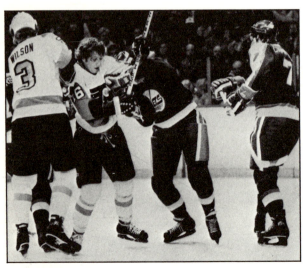

High sticks, tie-ups, and bloodied faces result from Philadelphia's rough style of play.

Reggie Leach and others managed to kill off 79 percent of the Flyer penalties without allowing a goal. At the same time, they led the league in scoring 15 shorthanded goals.

Statistics indicate that your team is superior to the North Stars. This is the Flyer team that set an NHL record by playing in 35 straight games without a loss! Your regular season record of 48 wins, 12 losses, and 20 ties far overshadows the North Stars' mark of 36 wins, 28 losses, and 16 ties. Veterans such as Reggie Leach (50 goals), Bill Barber (40 goals), and the great all-around player Clarke give you a huge advantage over the North Stars in pressure games.

What's Your Decision?

You are the coach.
You must beat the North Stars to make the Stanley Cup finals.
What is your game strategy for the rest of the series?

#1 Will you try to avoid giving the North Stars power plays and rely on your superior experience, depth, and all-around skill to overcome Minnesota's skating?

#2 Will you risk the attack and try to rattle the young Stars with your aggressive checking, counting on your penalty-killers to bail you out?

Choose the strategy. Then turn the page to find out which strategy the Flyers' coach chose.

The Flyers decided on #2.

They wanted to force the North Stars into timid play by checking them aggressively. For one thing, Philadelphia felt that the play-offs were no time to experiment with a new style of play. The Flyers had always relied on a checking game. Also, they felt that their opponents' inexperience made them especially vulnerable to the added pressure of an aggressive team. Philadelphia hoped that they could dash the North Stars' confidence enough so that Minnesota's power play would be ineffective.

Here's What Happened!

The result of this decision was obvious in the very next game. Minnesota enjoyed seven power play advantages but managed only 7 shots on goal during them and did not score a goal. Philadelphia won, 7 to 0.

In game number three, the North Stars made one goal in eight power play chances. But even that was offset when Bill Barber scored a shorthanded goal. The Flyers won again, 5 to 3.

During the next two games, the North Stars had no better luck. They went 14 straight power plays without putting a puck in the net and allowed Barber to score shorthanded again. Philadelphia turned what could have been a difficult series into an easy 4 games to 1 triumph.

Barber scored a Stanley Cup record of three shorthanded goals in a series. With players like Barber and a team that at one point stopped 26 of 27 Minnesota power plays, Philadelphia could afford to play aggressively. The North Stars were thrown off their skating game and were never able to challenge the Flyers.

Next page: Flyer goal-scoring leader Reggie Leach jostles for position against a North Star defender and goalie Gilles Meloche. Philadelphia outmuscled Minnesota throughout their series to advance to the Stanley Cup finals.

9 The Man Without a Stick

Islander players look on in frustration as Philadelphia's good
luck strikes again in the form of a Flyer goal.

You are coaching
the Philadelphia Flyers.

You've just beaten the Minnesota North Stars to gain a spot in the 1980 Stanley Cup final round. In this series, you're pitted against the New York Islanders, a team that after four outstanding seasons of play has at last made it into the Stanley Cup finals.

It often takes a little luck to win a championship, and luck seems to have been wearing a Philadelphia Flyer uniform for most of this game. An example of this extraordinary luck occurred in the opening game of this series. In the first period, the Islanders scored your first goal! New York's defensive ace, Denis Potvin, accidentally helped guide the puck into his own net.

Then, with the score tied at 2-2 in the third period, your center, Rick MacLeish, shot from an almost hopeless angle. Again, luck prevailed. The puck somehow sneaked past Islander goalie Billy Smith.

You still held a one-goal lead late in the period when your forward, Al Hill, was sent off the ice for a two-minute penalty. Your Flyer penalty killers had been skating away the time nicely when luck suddenly jumped to the Islanders. Your Bill Barber, who had helped you reach the finals with his tremendous series against Minnesota, broke his stick while defending against New York. The game isn't going to stop while Barber gets a new stick. What should you do? Consider your situation.

The rule book makes three basic points about broken-stick situations.

1. Any player who breaks his stick may still participate in the action as long as he drops what is left of his stick.
2. A player other than a goalie may not receive a stick from a teammate on the ice. He must skate to the bench to pick up a new stick.
3. A two-minute penalty plus a 10-minute misconduct penalty is charged to any player violating rule 2.

If Barber happened to be on the bench side of the rink, your choice would be easier. He could just rush over, grab a new stick, and continue playing. But both Bill and the puck are clear across the ice. The Islanders have just gained control of the puck and are starting towards your goal.

Your Flyers could help out Barber by forcing a face-off. If they could freeze the puck against the boards or flip it into the crowd, the action would stop and Barber could get a new stick. Your team is quite good at stopping the action, especially when it comes to trapping the puck in the corners. During this game, there has been an average of one face-off every 50 seconds.

If your team could just swat the puck back down the ice, it would give Barber enough time to get a stick. But you are up against a slick-passing

88

Islander power play and it will not be easy to get the puck away from them. Although each of the Islander stars—Bryan Trottier, Mike Bossy, Clark Gillies, and Denis Potvin—fell off in their goal production this year, they are still a dangerous group. All can pass, stickhandle, and shoot.

The most deadly shooter is Bossy, New York's top goal scorer with 51 goals. Bossy gets his shots away quickly and rarely shoots wide of the net. Center Trottier may be the top all-around forward in the game. This season he scored 42 goals and 62 assists and he has been hot in the play-offs as well. Burly Clark Gillies adds muscle and a season total of 19 goals, 35 assists to the attack.

Clark Gilles   Mike Bossy

Stefan Persson   Denis Potvin

Potvin and Stefan Persson man the points on the power play. They station themselves just inside the blue line and keep the puck in the attacking zone. Due to injuries, Potvin has played only 31 games this season, but he seems to be back near full strength now. Persson, a Swedish-born player, has scored only four goals but is an expert at moving the puck around to his teammates.

Your team has always been good at killing off penalties. In the previous chapter, you relied on them to overcome the North Stars' power play. Besides having excellent checkers such as Barber and Bobby Clarke, you also have several sets of good, tough defensemen.

During the 1979-80 season, Philadelphia center Rick MacLeish contributed 31 goals and 35 assists.

What's Your Decision?

You are the coach.

You have half a minute to go before Hill comes out of the penalty box to put your team at full strength. Meanwhile, the Islanders are rushing toward your net with the puck.

What should you do?

#1 Wave Barber to the bench to come and get another stick.

#2 Let Barber stay on the ice and play without a stick.

#3 Take the penalty and get a stick to Barber.

Choose the play. Then turn the page to find out which play the Flyers' coach chose.

The Flyers went with choice #2.

The coach allowed Barber to stay on the ice even though he didn't have a stick. It would have taken Bill several seconds to skate over to the bench and back to his position. With the Islanders on the attack, those seconds could make the difference between a goal and a missed shot. It was decided that Barber should try to defend without a stick until a better opportunity came for getting a new one.

Here's What Happened!

Potvin moved in to attack for the Islanders. He slid the puck over to Bossy near the boards. Bossy spotted Persson moving in unguarded from the other side. He fed a pass to Persson, who then, with only 17 seconds left in the penalty, sent the puck past Philadelphia goalie Pete Peeters. Barber later said that if only he had had a stick, he might have been able to tip Bossy's pass away from Persson.

The goal tied the score and sent the game into overtime. Two minutes into the sudden-death period, Philadelphia found itself on the wrong end of a controversial decision. New York's John Tonelli moved in for a shot and was dragged down by the Flyers' Jimmy Watson. Watson was expecting that the officials would ignore more penalties during the overtime period, as was usually the case. But the penalty was called, and Watson went off the ice for two minutes.

One second remained in Watson's penalty when Potvin drilled a goal for a 4 to 3 win on the Flyers' rink. New York went on to win the series, four games to two.

10 Team U.S.A. Meets "The Soviet System"

Can the young Americans match the experienced Soviets and
their brand of swift skating and smooth puck handling?

You are coaching
the United States Olympic team.

For a hockey team that was rated the seventh best in this 1980 Olympic competition, you have pulled off some major surprises so far. Thanks to a frantic, last-minute rally, you tied Sweden in your first game and went on to shock Czechoslovakia 7 to 3 in the next game. You are undefeated going into the final medal round, but almost no one expects the upsets to continue. The reason for this is that your next opponent is a team that is considered the best in the world—the Soviet Union. You learned firsthand how good the Soviets are when they thrashed you 10-3 in an exhibition just before the Olympics.

You have been drilling your team in a style of play that North American players are not used to. You hope these drills will help the U.S. team combat the fast European style of play. But as the tense Olympic contest with the Soviets began, this style didn't seem to do much good. Through two periods, the Soviets outplayed you easily. Only some extremely lucky breaks have kept you within one goal of them, with the score at 3 to 2.

During the last period it sometimes seemed as though the Soviets were toying with you. As you head into the final period with a chance for a great upset, you wonder whether you should stay with this new system of play or go back to a more familiar style.

Some Key Team U.S.A. Players

Bill Baker

Neal Broten

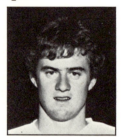

Dave Christian

Mike Eruzione

Mark Johnson

Jack O'Callahan

Rob McClanahan

Ken Morrow

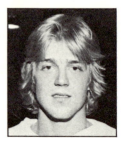

Eric Strobel

Review the main differences in the two styles of play.

Dump-and-run vs. puck control. The professional style of play in North America consists largely of carrying the puck to the opponent's blue line and firing it into the corners. Then the players chase after the puck, hoping to dig it away from the boards and from the opponents.

Would the North American strategy of dumping the puck into an opponent's offensive zone and digging after it along the boards—demonstrated here by a Buffalo Sabre— be successful against the faster Russians?

97

The European-style game that the Soviets play demands that you keep control of the puck. Rather than fire the puck into the corners, you carry it or pass it into the offensive zone.

Position vs. puck control. North American coaches have usually been strict about players keeping their positions on the ice. Wings are supposed to patrol their section of ice and not go skating all over the rink. But you have been trying to impress upon your players that, again, control of the puck is more important than maintaining position.

Deft puck control is a hallmark of the Soviet style of play. Can you rely on your players to beat the Russians at their own game?

There are several reasons why you might want to stay with your new style.

An Olympic rink is larger than a North American hockey rink. This allows more room for maneuvering and passing and demands skill over muscle. Europeans are so quick at breaking out of their defensive end that it is not easy to pressure them into mistakes.

Even though you have been outplayed, you have done better than most people expected. You are only one goal behind. And because of a fluke goal, the Soviets' top goalie was yanked out of the game.

You might want to think twice about changing from your system when you have been drilling it into your players for six grueling months. Your team has played over 60 games during that time and has won most of them. That is far better than U.S.A. teams of the past have done using the North American tactics.

Your team has shown that it has the conditioning needed to make this type of strategy work. You have pushed your players hard, often skating them for an hour <u>after</u> a game. So far during the Olympics, you have gotten stronger as the game has gone on. You've outscored your foes 11 to 3 in third-period action.

It is tempting, however, to switch back to the old style.

The close score could hardly be more deceiving. The Soviets' three goals were well earned. Your two goals were largely gifts of fortune. The first was on a 50-foot shot by Buzz Schneider. The second was even more of a fluke. Dave Christian blasted a long shot from center ice as the period was about to end. The Soviet goalie had only to sweep the shot to the side and the period would have been over. But he let it bounce directly to Mark Johnson who pushed it past him with one second left.

A look at the shot totals confirms the Soviets' dominance. In the first period, you were outshot 18 to 8. In the second period, you hardly tested the new Soviet goalie as you managed only 2 shots to the Soviets' 12.

You must remember that the Soviet Union has been playing this wide-open, passing type of game longer than you have. Perhaps you are playing into their hands by adopting a style similar to theirs. Finally, you must debate the sense of trying to outlast the Soviets with the demanding style of play. The Soviets are world famous as an incredibly well-conditioned team. Earlier in this Olympics, they showed their form against Finland. The Finns led 2 to 1 with five minutes left, but the Soviets unleashed a quick, three-goal burst and won the game. As you make your decision, you are aware that your players are up against the team that won the last four hockey gold medals.

Olympic Games Hockey History

YEAR	GOLD MEDAL	SILVER MEDAL	BRONZE MEDAL
1920	Canada	United States	Czechoslovakia
1924	Canada	United States	Great Britain
1928	Canada	Sweden	Switzerland
1932	Canada	United States	Germany
1936	Great Britain	Canada	United States
1948	Canada	Czechoslovakia	Switzerland
1952	Canada	United States	Sweden
1956	USSR	United States	Sweden
1960	United States	Canada	USSR
1964	USSR	Sweden	Czechoslovakia
1968	USSR	Czechoslovakia	Canada
1972	USSR	United States	Czechoslovakia
1976	USSR	Czechoslovakia	West Germany

What's Your Decision?

You are the coach.
As you hear the shouts of "U-S-A!" echoing around the hockey arena, you must make your final strategy decision.
How will you proceed?

#1 Stay with your new system
#2 Go back to the more familiar one

Choose the strategy. Then turn the page to find out which strategy the Team U.S.A. coach chose.

Team U.S.A. stayed with #1.

Coach Herb Brooks fought off the urge to fall back on the familiar, and he stayed with his original plan.

Here's What Happened!

Team U.S.A. began to pressure the Soviets. Responding to the cheers from the home crowd at Lake Placid, New York, Team U.S.A. finally tied the score with 8:39 left to play on a power play goal by Mark Johnson.

Less than two minutes later, the United States team cruised back into the Soviet end. Mark Pavelich slid a pass to team captain Mike Eruzione who shot it into the net for the lead goal. For the next ten minutes, the young U.S. team held off the frustrated Soviets and finally sent the jubilant crowd home celebrating a 4 to 3 win. Then, in their final game, the United States team went on to score a come-from-behind victory over Finland and clinched the gold medal.

It's pandemonium in Lake Placid as the Americans celebrate their historic upset of the Russians.

ACKNOWLEDGMENTS

Photo credits: pp. 99, 100, Amateur Hockey Association; pp. 11 (bottom), 71, Denis Brodeur; pp. 16 (bottom left), 19 (bottom left), Buffalo Sabres; pp. 9, 27 (bottom right), 52, 53, Chicago Black Hawks; pp. 7, 15, Chicago Tribune; pp. 94, 103, Duomo/Paul J. Sutton; pp. 48, 50, 56-7, Graphic Artists; p. 27 (bottom left), Los Angeles Kings; p. 79, Minnesota North Stars; p. 11 (top), Montreal Canadiens; pp. 16 (bottom right), 19 (bottom right), 97, Ron Moscati/Buffalo Sabres; pp. 89, 90, New York Islanders; pp. 27 (top center), 72, 73, 74, New York Rangers; pp. 20, 27 (top right), 80, 84-5, 86, 91, Philadelphia Flyers; pp. 27 (top left), 36, 38, 40, 41, 46-7, 58, 60, 66, 67, 68, Al Ruelle; pp. 19 (top), 24, 29, 34, 35, Robert B. Shaver; pp. 27 (bottom center), 42, St. Louis Blues; p. 16 (top), Bill Wippert/Buffalo Sabres; pp. 12, 76, Wide World Photos, Inc.

Cover photograph: Joe Bereswill

Also by Nate Aaseng

BASEBALL: YOU ARE THE MANAGER
10 exciting championship games

BASKETBALL: YOU ARE THE COACH
10 exciting NBA play-off games

FOOTBALL: YOU ARE THE COACH
10 exciting NFL play-off games

Lerner Publications Company
241 First Avenue North, Minneapolis, MN 55401